Author's Note: The informat
be used as a point of referer
stroll through the woods, or attempts to climb a mountain, does so
at his or her risk. Be safe my friends, and leave no trace....

Other Adirondack inspired novels by ERIN MAINE:

Bittersweet Justice

Masquerading Justice

Mystique River Justice

Murder in the Mountains

Moonlight Memories

***I am an organizer, and a planner. Sometimes, actually, most of the time, I over plan and overpack for a simple "day" hike. With that said, I would like to think that being ready for the unexpected is a very good motto to live by. The mountains are majestic, gorgeous and a great way to spend a day; but they also can be deadly... A few minutes of organizing and packing before your trip might very well save your life while on your hike or climb. There are many lists of what should be in your pack, the following 10 items are ALWAYS in my pack, whether it's a 2 mile walk in the woods, or a 15-mile climb.

My 10 "must have" items that can always be found in my pack:

1. Lighter, waterproof matches and lint, in a zip lock bag
2. Headlamp, with spare batteries (check it before you head out)
3. Food, (power bars, granola, lightweight but nutritious food)
4. Water (yes it weighs down your pack, but fill your water bladder up)
5. Base layer, and shell for rain
6. Fleece layering
7. Map, compass, hand-held GPS
8. Pocket/survival knife
9. Cellphone (make sure it's fully charge, & on low power mode, or off)
10. Military issue reflective blanket, and rope/twine

Last bit of "housekeeping" is the CODE OF HIKING CONDUCT:

-Leave no trace. Out of respect for our wildlife and others, if you carry it in, carry it out. Hike on the trails, and avoid walking on vegetation growing on the summit and along designated trails.

-Wear the right clothing and footwear. It is always a good idea to layer and in the hiking world, there is a sentiment that "cotton kills". Wear appropriate footwear, socks that wick moisture, and layer your attire. Ticks are on the rise in ADK's and long light colored pants, tucked into socks is recommended.

-Bring water & snacks, and plenty of them. Remember to bring a bowl/dish for any 4 legged friends that join you on your hike. Always bring more water than you think you'll need.

-Respect wildlife. You are in their environment; leave them alone! If you see a wild animal, observe them from a distance. Don't ever attempt to follow or chase any wildlife. What looks like an adorable baby might have a very protective momma roaming very near by.

The term "Go Take A Hike" means many things to many people. For me, it's not about the summit, standing atop the firetower, catching the fish at some secret fishing hole or being the fastest to reach the peak. It's about the journey getting there.

My parents might not have had a lot of extra money to purchase the fanciest of outdoor gear, nor did they take us camping in the largest camper available. In fact, the oldest memories that I have of camping took place in my Uncle Albert's old Army tent, complete with ropes jutting out of the weathered canvas every couple feet or so. At night, when nature called, I can remember more than one swear word permeating the air as someone tripped over the corded twine, or stubbed their toe on the old wooden stakes sticking out of the hardened soil. It was a monster to not only put up but to walk inside. The interior was hot with stagnant air trapped inside a windowless monstrosity of what would become my sleeping headquarters for two weeks every summer. My sister Beth, and my cousin Rita and her best friend Sue, would always fight over what was the highest ground in the tent, hoping that our summer vacation wouldn't be interrupted by rain and the subsequent deluge of water that always seemed to make its' way through the tent. I can remember plenty of occasions looking down from my wooden army cot, as the endless stream of water made its way through the sand and out the other side. In retrospect, if the walls of that old battered tent could talk, I'd be the first one to spend another weekend inside it to hear her stories. By the time I hit adolescence, I thought we were rich as my parents were finally able to purchase a little Scotty camper for our annual adventure. I don't think it was more than ten feet long, but to me it was nirvana and when not camping, I'd spent countless hours in it as it sat surrounded by pines in our back yard. It was in that second-hand Scotty trailer that I developed my love of writing.

Our parents always took us to the same state run campground year after year. It was at Fish Creek, north of Tupper Lake, that my love of the mountains was formed. Even though I spent majority of my childhood helping my father cut, stack and load firewood into our cellar to heat the tiny house that I grew up in; it wasn't until we had the great fortune of meeting The Shaffer Family of Linwood, New Jersey that my love of the woods was cemented.

The Shaffer's had four children, all close in age to my sister and I. Robyn, their eldest daughter, and I immediately hit it off, despite a two year age difference. Her parents got along well with mine, so year after year we returned to the same camp ground, at the same time, eventually requesting side by side sites. My family introduced Robyn to our love of the water. Our canoe trips would originate at the boat launch within the campground, and meander through endless passages that never seemed to allow us to reach our destination. But as kids, we didn't care because we were too busy fishing, catching water lilies or frogs. We'd pull Ole Ironside (yes our canoe had a name, and a placard glued inside its' hull reminding us of the history of its' name) onto sand bars and swim while my mother would scold us for splashing her. Lunch always tasted better when enjoyed while on an adventure. We'd spend the entire day on the water and just when it seemed that we'd never reach our destination, the outlet for Rollins Pond would appear on the horizon, and my exhausted biceps would rejoice. I was a tom boy growing up, and always thought of myself as in excellent shape; but I'll admit, the sight of the boat launch and shoreline signaling the end of paddling was a welcome relief. Exhausted as we were when it ended, we were ready for the next adventure upon rising the following day. That's where the Shaffer's stepped in.

Mr. and Mrs. Shaffer enjoyed a different element of the Adirondacks, one that can only be witnessed from up above, where birds fly. They loved to climb mountains. I can not recall all of the names of the summits I scaled with them, nor can I tell you which high peaks we conquered first or last; but I can say that each one was an adventure and amazing in its' own right. I can clearly remember my mother packing my backpack with DEET, Band-Aids, my dad's old army canteen for water, a couple peanut butter sandwiches (I don't like PB & J), a few homemade cookies, my favorite bandana (if I wasn't already wearing it around my neck or on my head holding back my mop of hair), some rolled up twine, an ace wrap, and an extra pair of socks. My dad would always slip me a cigarette lighter for my pack as well, making sure my mother didn't see him as he tucked it inside my pack. We never had any of the fancy hiking gear that the Sears & Roebuck catalog displayed, but even so, we still were somewhat prepared for our journey. The one memory that I recall from each hike was that every hiker, despite our age or size, was responsible for carrying his or her own pack. I think this was Mr. Shaffer's subtle way of instilling in each of us that we are responsible for ourselves. The one exception that I remember was when Robyn slipped on the summit of Haystack and Mr. Shaffer and Robyn's older brother Johnny had to carry her down the trail the entire way. She was given a pass that day.

The Shaffers didn't just trudge up mountains to reach the summit. As educators, the woods became their classroom, with them teaching us about the trees, the flora and fauna surrounding the path. I remember learning about wild mushrooms, the animals indigenous to the area, how to read the multi-colored trail markers, and the weather. They taught us how to use a compass and how to read the sky, always searching for signs of impending hail storms or lightening. I'm the first to admit, I still have difficulty using a compass, but thanks in part to my New Jersey family, I never feel lost in the woods.

You don't have to tackle Mount Marcy on your first adventure outside. Go to your neighborhood park and bring your kids, and your imagination. Our children are our greatest accomplishments;

help them create memories that will last a lifetime. Time spend away from TV's and cellphones is time well spent. So, visit a State Park, go on a drive in the countryside bird watching, sit by a babbling brook and read; just do it! And when you can't think of anything to do, GO TAKE A HIKE!

HAPPY HIKING!!!

ADIRONDACK PARK FIRE TOWER CHALLENGE: You must complete all 5 Catskill Towers, and 18 of the 23 Adirondack Towers to complete this challenge. The towers are as follows and not in order of difficulty:

Azure	Hadley	Overlook
Bald	Hunter	Pillsbury
Balsam	Hurricane	Poke-o-moonshine
Belfry	Kane	Red Hill
Black	Lyon	Snowy
Blue	Mount Adams	Spruce
Cathedral	Mount Arab	St Regis
Goodnow	Mount Tremper	Vanderwhacker
Gore	Owls Head	Wakely, Woodhull

Hike the Adirondacks and become a Saranac Lake 6er!!!

A great way to introduce your children into hiking is by completing the Saranac Lake 6. Not only will your kids love getting their very own Saranac 6er patch, but hopefully, they'll fall in love with the mountains. There is no time limit for how long it takes to complete the 6 climbs. To become an "Ultra 6er, you must complete all 6 and then ring the 6er bell in Saranac Lake within a 24 hour window. The hikes comprising the Saranac Lake 6 are:

McKenzie   Ampersand   Scarface

Haystack   St Regis   Baker

If conquering 6 mountains seems like too much of a feat for your little ones, or 4 legged friends, start with THE TUPPER LAKE TRIAD:

The whole family needs to climb Arab, Coney and lastly Goodman, during the summer or winter season, in order to earn a patch (climb all 3 during different seasons and get both summer and winter patches).

The following are 100+ nature walks, hikes, mountain climbs, and strolls to waterfalls & fishing holes. Some will be great picnic areas, places to read a book or simply close your eyes and enjoy nature at its' finest. All will provide excellent photo opportunities and are guaranteed to be worth it.

They are in alphabetical order and not in order by distance or difficulty. Again, they are a guide only; and each person utilizing this book must be responsible for their own health and ability. Don't risk it if you have doubts about your stamina and ability to complete the hike. Don't become a DEC search & rescue, or worse, a statistic.

HAPPY HIKING!!

AUGER FLATS & FALLS RIVER WALK

Getting There: From Speculator, head out of town towards Wells on Route 8/30. Continue approximately 6.5 miles to Old Route 8 on the left. Park at the bridge.

The Hike: Starting at Old Route 8, cross the bridge and take the immediate right, crossing a small wooded bridge over a creek. The trail now opens up and crosses several small rolling hills. Auger Flats is on your right signified by a very slow moving current. When you reach the gorge, if traveling with young children, please use caution as the ledges are very steep and can be slippery.

Auger Falls Trail Eastside: from NY 8, walk ½ mile along the one lane dirt road (Teachout Road) and cross the bridge at Griffin Gorge. Past the bridge, turn left, to Auger Falls Way. The land surrounding the road is privately so please be respectful. Please don't trespass past the trees with yellow paint marking the boundaries. Walk ½ mile and go past barrier at the end of the road.

*The easy hike earns you 1 point on the ADK Waterfall Challenge.

AUSTIN FALLS

Getting There: Drive North on Route 30 out of Wells. Continue to the intersection of Rte 30 & 8. From that point, continue another 6.5 miles, making a right onto Old Route 30, and drive 2.7 miles on the rough road. Pull off to the side of the road where you find parking. The road is accessible to all vehicles but is very rough and bumpy so use caution. The falls can be heart from the road.

The Hike: No working up a sweat required as the hike is an easy 50 foot walk down to the falls. The view is breathtaking, but use caution when walking alongside the falls as the banks may be very slippery.

*Note: The 50 foot walk not only is enjoyable but also counts towards the ADK Waterfall Challenge and is worth 1 point!

BAKER MOUNTAIN

Getting There: From downtown Saranac Lake, follow Main Street until the intersection of Dugway, turning right onto Dugway and taking it to the end. Then take a left onto Forest Hill Avenue proceeding straight to Moody Pond on your right, trailhead on your left.

The Hike: Easy, quick and only 0.9 miles long, this cute little mountain is often climbed following a longer, more strenuous hike. It is the shortest of the 6 mountains comprising the Saranac Lake 6er Challenge. Steep only in a few sections, you will be astounded at the views this 2452 foot summit afford. The elevation gain is only 900 feet, making this a very popular hike in the Saranac Lake area.

BALSAM LAKE MOUNTAIN

Getting there: Located in Hardenburgh in the Catskill Mountains, there are numerous trails leading to the summit. The easiest route is the Old road to the fire tower.

The Hike: The most frequently used approach is via Mill Brook Road and follows an old jeep road to the fire tower. The summit can be reached at 3,720 feet and the tower only adds to the amazing views that can be found at the end of this attractive, family friendly hike.

BASFORD FALLS

Getting There: From Cranberry Lake, Take Route 3 out of town. Turn onto Tooley Pond Road and approximately 15.3 miles from NY3. The road can be winding at time. This is a very good one to do in conjunction with Sinclair Falls as you will pass Sinclair Falls ½ mile before the parking area for Basford Falls. There is a white DEC sign, marking the start of the trail.

The Hike: Once parked, the trail is an old logging road to start, turning into a hiking trail as you get closer to the river. Bring a picnic basket or fishing pole as this is a great little hike to enjoy a few hours at.

BEACH MILL POND TRAIL (GLEASMANS FALLS)

Getting there: From Utica, head 1 hour north on Route 12 to Lowville. Turn east on River Road and proceed approximately four miles to the town of Watson. From there, turn onto the Number Four Road and go approximately 2.7 miles until you find Loson Road. Go approximately 4/10 mile and turn right onto McPhilmy Road crossing Erie Canal Road and proceed on the dirt road. (sounds difficult but all roads up until this point are marked). Lastly, turn left onto Beach Mill Road which may or may not show up on your GPS. Take this road three miles to trailhead parking. You will find a barrier in front of you upon arrival. (make sure where road splits and you see Cleveland Lake Road going off to the right, you veer left as this is the road you're looking for.

The Hike: Give yourself enough time to enjoy and not rush, but keep in mind that the hike to the falls is 2.9 miles one way. From the trailhead, you note that you start off by descending into the creek bank and crossing the creek. Make sure you register before going any further. After registering, the road will take you toward Beach Mill Pond. It is a well used trail and easy to follow.

Once at the falls, the trail does, in fact continue for another 4+ miles and ends over the Independence River.

BEAVER MEADOW FALLS

Getting there: From I-87 Northway, exit 30 onto NY 9. Approximately 2.4 miles, go through intersection and continue on NY 73 toward Lake Placid. Slow down at 5.6 miles, turn left onto gravel road leading to the Ausable Club (main club entrance is 0.5 miles further down the road). There is a dedicated parking area. NOTE: The trailhead for the AMR will be on the right, across the road from the Roaring Brook Falls Trail.

The Hike: From the parking lot, there is a dirt road which leads to a paved road. Just before the main club house for the Ausable Club, turn left between the tennis courts to get to the gate into the AMR. (AMR is private but allows hikers recreational easements). From the gate, hike the dirt road approximately 2 miles to a sign for a trail both Gothics and Beaver Meadows Falls.

Once you cross the Ausable River, you will hear the falls before you see it! Beaver Meadow Falls is considered to be one of the most picturesque falls in all of the ADKs and although only 60 feet high, it truly is breath taking. If traveling with young children, be sure to pack plenty of snacks and maybe a dry pair of shoes. The mist off the falls can make for a soggy walk back.

Fun Fact: Based on the water level, it is possible to stand beneath the falls for not only some cool pictures but also a refreshing shower.

BELFRY MOUNTAIN

Getting There: From the Northway, take Exit 30, turning south on NY 9 for only 0.1 mile. Make a quick turn left onto Essex Cty Rte 6/Tracy Road. There will be a sign for Witherbee & Port Henry. Continue approx. 7.5 miles to a 4 way intersection. Turn left onto Route 70 and continue just 0.1 miles to roadside parking on the right (look for bright yellow steel gate on the left). It is easy to miss the DEC trailhead so go slow and be on the lookout for a state trail sign on the side of the road (near an iron gate) and a large pile of rocks near the entrance gives the appearance of a rock quarry.

 GPS coordinates are N44 06.139 W73 32.780.

The Hike: For anyone with small children, or someone looking to bag another firetower while in the area, this is the perfect hike for you. The summit can be found after meandering along a gravel access road for the first 2/10th of a mile, and then conquering the summit just a few minutes later. This quick hike is a short .30 or .35 mile long (depending on who you believe), and only has an elevation gain of less than 140 feet, it is a very easy hike and there quite possibly isn't another hike in NY State that offers such a panoramic view for such little effort. This little mountain definitely offers a big bang for a few minutes' work of walking! When on top of the 1840-foot summit, Lake Champlain, Schroon Lake, Marcy, The Green Mountains of Vermont and many other high peaks are visible to the naked eye. Be on the lookout for a state trail sign on the side of the road (near an iron gate) and a large pile of rocks near the entrance gives the appearance of a rock quarry.

Fun Fact: This half hour hike still counts towards the Firetower Challenge and although it almost seems like cheating, it's okay because other hikes in the ADK Firetower Challenge will make up for the energy you didn't need to exert with this one!

BLACK MOUNTAIN

Getting There: From Lake George, head south on Route 9 turning left onto Route 149. Take 149 until the intersection of Routes 4/22. Turn left onto 4/22 and continue until Whitehall, bearing left onto Route 22 at this point. Continue on Route 22 through the lower end of Lake Champlain. Make a left turn onto Route 6 toward Hullett's Landing, turning left onto Pike Brook Road. Once on Pike Brook Road, be on the lookout for the trailhead, approximately 1 mile down the road on the right hand side.

The Hike: The hike to the summit is quite easy for adults and children alike, with only a few challenging spots. The views from the summit are breathtaking, and the fire tower makes this hike part of the NY State Fire Tower Challenge. With the summit being mostly barren rock, and at 2665 feet, the summit affords great views in all directions. From the trailhead, expect to hike 2.8 miles to the Firetower, 6.2 if you do the Black Mountain Loop which is lightly trafficked but clearly marked and is not only dog friendly but kid friendly as well.

Fun Fact: For the more adventurous, Lapland Pond Lean-to can be found on your return leg of the loop and makes for a great place to sleep under the stars. Another fun fact: This fire tower was manned by fire wardens up until the 1970's.

BLACK BEAR MOUNTAIN

Getting There: Anyone who's ever spent any time in the Old Forge area, has probably heard of this cute day hike. Leaving Old Forge on Route 28, heading towards Inlet, the trailhead is very well marked and easily seen on the left, as you observe 4th Lake on your right. The parking area is large, with Rocky Point's trailhead located beside Black Bear's.

The Hike: The trail starts out nothing more than a peaceful walk in the woods, but will become relatively steeper as you approach a series of rock steps and finally the summit. The trail has a few areas that get muddy and mucky but has wooden bridges, and beams to circumvent these areas. The summit is rocky and allows a magnificent view of the surrounding mountains.

CARPENTER FALLS

Getting There: Take Route 20 towards Skaneateles to West Lake Road, a/k/a NY 41A. Head south down West Lake Road for approximately 11 miles. At the 11 mile mark, look for Apple Tree Road and head down it for ½ mile. There you will find a small parking lot on the left with a small kiosk information center.

The Hike: From the kiosk, Carpenter Falls is simply a 1/10th of a mile stroll down a well worn trail. (It is the trail to the left of the kiosk, with Angel Falls ½ mile away, down the right trail). Both are worth viewing as Carpenter Falls drops over 90 feet and Angel Falls is over 60 feet.

CATHEDRAL ROCK

Getting There: The trailhead is located approximately 8 miles West of Cranberry Lake. Take Route 3 out of town, turning onto Wanakena Road on the left. Follow Wanakena Road, making a left onto Ranger School road. Drive to the end of Arboretum Road, parking behind the Ranger School on the left by a huge open field (note: students park in the lot so it might appear very crowded).

The Hike: This very short hike is slightly longer than one mile and can easily be done in 2-3 hours round trip, even with small children. The overall elevation gain is less than 200 feet and the views from the fire tower on the summit are breathtaking. Note: Though the trail is very well marked and quite easy to navigate following the Latham Fire Tower Trail. If traveling with small children, be cognoscente of the steep cliffs near the summit.

Fun Fact: The fire tower on Cathedral Rock originally was on the summit of Tooley Pond Mountain and was moved by Ranger School Students in 1970.

CHIMNEY MOUNTAIN

Getting There: Located in the Central region of the Adirondacks, it's summit borders Hamilton and Warren counties. From Indian Lake, head south on Route 30 and turn onto Big Brook Road at mile 0.6. Continue southeast on Big Brook Road to the crossroad intersection of Hutchins and Moulton Roads at approximately 1.5 miles and then turn right following Big Brook Road. 2.2 miles down the road, there is an unmarked right hand turn. Then continue 2.5 miles from that turn to the end of the road at King's Flow (by a former Scout camp). There is a large parking area at The Cabins at Chimney Mountain (7.8 miles from Route 30).

The Hike: Chimney Mountain is only 2708 feet in elevation and can be hiked during all four seasons and is one of the most popular day hikes in the central Adirondacks. The summit offers 360 degree views and is only slightly longer than a mile in length, therefore making it accessible to all levels of hikers, from inexperienced first timers to seasoned veterans. The chimney and rock formations that can be found on the summit provide many opportunities for climbing and exploring, and the system of caves and rock crevasses are an added bonus.

Fun Facts: The true summit of the mountain is not where the chimney is located but actually a short hike to the right before the trail to the chimney, via a herd path. Also, the chimney formation is surrounded with multiple caves and crevices, all situated near the summit.

CHRISTINE FALLS

Getting There: This adorable falls and picnic area is a 5-minute walk. From the intersection of Route 30 & 8 in Speculator, follow 8 towards Wells. Continue approximately 3.6 miles to an unmarked access area below the dam on the left side of the road. There is a small dirt pull off behind the guardrails.

The Hike: The falls can be heard and practically seen from the parking area. The path to the falls is a rocky downhill slope overlooking the falls, and is less than 0.1 miles in duration. Family friendly hike but take caution as you approach the water.

COPPER ROCK FALLS

Getting There: From Cranberry Lake on NY 3, be on the lookout for Tooley Pond Road and is approx. 8 miles from NY3. Parking can be found on the shoulder but unfortunately, there isn't a DEC sign and can be easily missed.

The hike: Look for a small sign below a DEC Forest Preserve sign. Once you've found the trail, the scavenger hunt is over, as the trail itself is well worn, entering the forest quickly. The sound of the river can be heard from this point, and you'll find the river itself just a few steps away. At 0.2 miles, you'll come to a series of rapids, and believe it or not, you've reached the Copper Rock Falls. Continue on the trail, and soon you'll find a few more waterfalls come into view. If you can find the trailhead, this is an excellent picnic spot; and a very easy jaunt with children.

CRANE MOUNTAIN

Getting there: Take I-87 to Warrenburg/Diamond Point exit 23 off the Northway to US 9. Go only 0.8 miles and turn left onto Richards Ave. Cross over the river, turning onto NY 418W/River St. After 3.5 miles, turn right onto Athol Rd ,go another 3.5 miles, turn right again onto Mtn Rd. 5.5 miles to Thurman 3. Left onto Garnett Lake Rd/Co Road 72. In 1.2 miles, turn right onto Ski Hill Road. From the south: NY 8 to Johnsburg. Left onto Rte 57/South Johnburg Rd. In Thurman, turn right onto 72/Garnet Lake Rd. Right onto Ski Hill Road. GPS coordinates are N43 32.250 W73 58.084

The Hike: There are two options for reaching the summit with the 1st being a quick 1.4 mile ascent with an elevation change of 1150 feet. The 2nd option (and th one more suitable for those traveling with young children) takes a loop hike and reaches the summit in a little over 3 miles. The shorter, more direct route to the summit is comprised of rocks and scrambling along the way in a few spots, with shoes with good traction being a must for this hike (and most hikes). Near the summit, there are two vertical ladders that need to be climbed to reach the summit, with the longer ladder being 30 feet in length and might not be the best idea for the person with a fear of heights. The ladders are bolted into place and very solid, but are intimidating to look at!

Fun Fact: Bring your fishing rod! There is excellent fishing in the pond found on the trail!

FALLS ON THE WEST BRANCH OF SACANDAGA RIVER

Getting There: From Wells NY, follow Route 30 South, turning onto Algonquin Road. Follow Algonquin Road to West River Road, which is 0.7 miles past the dam. Take West River Road approximately 8.4 miles to a large clearing at the end of the road.

The Hike: The trail starts in the woods, paralleling the river most of the way to the falls. This 5 mile round trip is enjoyable and should be taken when the water levels are low. Before you reach the West Branch Falls, you will cross Cold Brook at approximately 1.9 miles and can see Cold Brook Falls directly upstream. Follow the river on the north bank until you see the 1st set of waterfalls on the West Branch. There is a smaller second falls a few hundred yards up the river but is difficult to access and not recommended.

Note: Much of this hike is on uneven terrain and caution should be used if traveling with children as the gorge drop off is over 400 feet in some places.

*This hike is part of the ADK Waterfall Challenge.

FORT NOBLE MOUNTAIN

Getting there: Located near Dolgeville NY, the parking for this long forgotten former fire tower is located right on Route 8, approximately 2 miles east of the Nobleboro bridge crossing the West Canada Creek, just east of the county line. The designated parking area can be seen off to the left but don't go looking for a trailhead sign because you won't find one!

The hike: The beginning of the trail is very easy to follow, and well-traveled by hikers and fishermen alike. Follow it down to the river approximately 0.3 miles. Now it's decision time. There are old cables on the old what appear to be old bridge supports, but utilizing this mode of crossing the water is not recommended nor encouraged and should be done so at one's own risk. The most reliable way is to ford the creek, and after climbing the bank, the trail is much less distinct but still easy to follow. After several hundred yards of climbing, you might see a decrepit shack but the overgrowth in the area makes it hard to see. At this point the trail bares left, crossing an often wet area. From there, you will start to climb very steeply. You'll know the summit is near once you go up some old stone steps and find a fern meadow. Even though the fire tower was removed a few decades ago, not that this quick jaunt ranks as the 728th highest mountain in New York State, and getting to the summit can be an adventure in and of itself!

Fun Fact: The mountain is only 2310 feet in elevation but with the obstacles to make it to the summit, might rank up there with many high peaks in testing one's endurance.

GIANT MOUNTAIN

Getting There: From Lake Placid, heading toward Keene Valley, Giant Mountain parking area can be found on Route 73. Drive through Keene and Keene Valley and past

Saint Huberts. Look for Chapel Pond on your right, the trailhead is just past the pond on your left. (Many times, Giant is often climbed with Rocky Peak Ridge)

The Hike: There actually are four major routes, with each offering a great hike. The Primary Trailhead is located at the St Huberts parking area/trailhead. This is a 6-mile round trip hike, that offers the opportunity to get your heart pumping as it is a steep ascent, and the most direct route to the summit. Even when your heart is racing, take the time to take in the sights, during this gorgeous hike. The views are endless, especially along the ridge and Giant Washbowl.

Secondary Trailhead: Leave LP on Route 73, follow toward Keene, again toward Saint Huberts, the trailhead for Giant and Rocky Falls is located across Route 73 from the AMR parking, approximately 3 miles outside of Keene Valley. This is a 7.2-mile hike round trip, and like the Primary Trailhead, you start climbing immediately upon leaving your car. Note: Giant is the 12th highest in the Adirondack range, and not recommended as a hike with young children. With an elevation of 4627, this High Peak offers spectacular views.

Fun Fact: Giant's original name was "Giant of the Valley".

GOOD LUCK LAKE & CLIFFS

Getting there: Located in the southern Adirondacks, the trailhead is less than 10 minutes north of the intersection of Route 29A and Route 10, heading north on 10 toward Speculator. The trail head will be located approximately 7 miles north on the left, and is just north of Canada Lake.

The Hike: Though the 5.1 mile hike is considered difficult, it is suitable for children and dogs alike with special precaution needed near the outcroppings of the cliffs. The elevation gain is 1056 feet and promises to provide an increase in one's heart rate, though the initial ¾ mile is Adirondack flat and only a gradual incline. At this point, the path to Good Luck Lake and its' subsequent camping sites can be found branching off to the left.

To get to the cliffs, look for the blue trail markers off to the right of the main trail, and just before a large wooden bridge, and subsequent snowmobile signs. Once the ascent is started, the 6/10 of a mile climb will feel longer than it is but once the granite cliffs are ascended, the views to the South-West will not disappoint.

Fun Facts: Spectacle Lake can be seen from the summit of Good Luck Cliffs and truly looks like a pair of glasses when viewed from above.

GOODNOW MOUNTAIN

Getting there: Route 28 North from Long Lake approximately 11 miles toward Newcomb. There is a ESF Trailhead sign on the right hand side of the road and ample parking.

The Hike: The trail is well used but also well maintained, compliments of the students at ESF. The hike is an easy 3.9 mile round trip hike, perfect for even the youngest adventurers. The total elevation change is only 1000, and from the tower's cabin, you will be able to enjoy a wonderful view of the High Peaks, and learn about the history of the mountain and its' namesake. Make sure to check out the huge tree growing over a massive boulder that can be found approximately 0.8 miles from the parking area. It will make for a great photo op. There are numerous wooden boardwalks along the well-worn path up the mountainside. At 1.6 there is an old barn, that once housed the fire ranger's horses. Once the summit is reached, the 60-foot fire tower emerges. It was erected in 1922 and staffed until 1970. Having made it to the summit, it is a must to climb the tower as the views from the cab are amazing with many high peaks visible.

Fun Facts: Goodnow Mountain was named after a homesteader who lived at the base of the mountain in the 1820's. The elevation at the summit is 2685 feet. There are 114 bird species that call the Adirondacks home and many can be found along the trail leading to the summit.

GREAT GULLY

Getting There: Located near the shores of Cayuga Lake, this is a great, kid-friendly walk. The area is ripe with birds and fun things to do, and very easy to get to. From the thruway, take NY 34 South out of Auburn. Once you reach the village of Fleming, turn onto 34B, southbound. Continue on 34B for 5 minutes until you see Great Gully Road (Route 89) on the right-hand side.   Take Route 89 for four miles until you see NY 90 (not the thruway 90). Turn left onto 90 and go only 3/10ths of a mile until you turn left onto a dirt lane, that is unmarked and has a small parking area.

The Hike: From the parking lot, take the dirt road toward the creek and before you know it, you'll see the first waterfall.   Within minutes, you'll find a very small waterfall, not to be confused with the one you're looking for. Backtrack a few steps, and continue on the well-worn dirt road and start a gradual climb toward the top of the falls. To reach the falls, you will be required to actually descend into the creek so be prepared for slightly wet feet. It is only a 6/10th of a mile walk to Great Gully Falls. Even with wet feet, this quick jaunt will be worth it.

HADLEY MOUNTAIN

Getting There: From the Northway, take exit 21 to NY 9, heading south.   You may also take 9N from Corinth, crossing the Hudson River into the village of Hadley. Turn onto Saratoga Route 1 and proceed approximately 3 miles to Hadley Hill Road on your left. The road will wind uphill for approximately 4.6 miles to Tower Road (look for a small sign) with turn on your right. Note: Tower Road is generally plowed in the winter making it accessible all four seasons. There is a large trailhead parking lot on the left.

At the end of the lake, the road A good workout, awesome views, and great open areas to enjoy a much-deserved lunch or tanning opportunity on any one of the numerous flat rocks. The summit elevation is 2675 with an elevation change of 1525 feet, making this a family friendly hike. There are no overly steep sections, nor tricky areas requiring scrambling on rocks. And with the numerous open areas along the trail, there are plenty of places to stop to enjoy the scenery or take a rest stop.

Fun Fact: Hadley is a sign of resilience and strength of Mother Nature. The West Mountain Range has burnt not once, but four different times since the turn of the 20th century. Hadley Mountain is the highest peak in the range and was not spared but has regrown much of its' forest after every fire.

HARPER FALLS

Getting There: Check out this adorable waterfalls in conjunction with Lampson Falls which is minutes away. From Cranberry Lake on NY 3 to Route 27 (approximately 16-17 miles from town). Once on 27, turn onto Donnerville Road, which is a seasonal gravel road, and proceed approximately 0.6 miles. Look for the DEC sign, which is located next to the parking area.

The Hike: Proceed to a yellow stop gate from the parking lot. From there, the trail will follow an old road approximately 6/10th of a mile. It is there that you'll reach a designated campsite and directly in front of you will be the Grass River. The trail meanders for about two miles along the river and offers several nice picnic areas or places for young ones to get their toes wet.

INMAN GULF

Getting There: Located near Barnes Corner, just west of Lowville. Take Route 177 out of Lowville, and look for the signs as soon as you pass through Barnes Corners. This 300 foot gorge is well worth the drive.

The Hike: There are miles of trails, but the 2.5 mile trail to the west has the best views and is moderate in grade. Bring your camera and enjoy nature at its finest. You will find breathtaking views, benches to rest on, and quiet solitude much of the year.

ITHACA FALLS NATURAL AREA

Getting there: From Route 13 in Ithaca, take Seneca Street east, turning left on Stewart Avenue and follow it into the Cornell University Campus and turn left onto University Ave. Left onto Lake street and then follow it to the right. Ithaca Falls will be on the right but the parking area is before the falls.

The Hike: Ithaca Falls offers multiple cascades and can be enjoyed year round. The falls itself is 105 feet high and nearly 180 feet wide at its' widest point. The falls is fed by Fall Creek which originates 8 miles away ear Fillmore Glen State Park and Summer Hill State Forest. As the flow can be very aggressive, especially during the spring thaw, swimming is strictly prohibited.

Walking to the falls takes less than 15 minutes and minimal exertion. Pets are allowed but must be on a leash, as with most parks.

Fun Fact: At the top of the falls, there is a small dam which is a remnant from a bygone era when the falls was used to generate power.

JENKINS MOUNTAIN

Getting There: Head north out of Old Forge on 28 through Blue Mountain, toward Long Lake, and Tupper Lake. Turn north onto 30 after leaving Tupper Lake (where 3 and 30 divide), heading toward Lake Clear. Just north of Lake Clear, 86 & 30, you'll find Paul Smiths College on NY State 30 and one mile north of the college, you'll find their Visitor Interpretive Center. The trailhead for the mountain can be found there.

The Hike: Not a high peak by any means, Jenkins Mountain still promises to provide you with an excellent workout. You'll gain 850+/- feet elevation gain during your 4 mile hike to the summit. Bring a lunch and camera and be sure to enjoy the views of the surrounding mountains. From the Visitor Interpretive Center, cross the road and find the gated woods road on your right. The beginning of the hike is ADK flat, with a descent before becoming ADK flat again. At this point, the trail makes a left and will pass beaver ponds and then the climbing begins.

KANE MOUNTAIN

Getting There: There are three ways to scale Kane Mountain but my preference is via the East Trail. Getting there is easy, and well-marked. Once in the village of Caroga Lake, turn off 10/29A onto Green Lake Road, (look for bridge crossing over Green Lake). If heading south, the turn off will be approximately 2 miles south of Pine Lake. Drive approximately 0.6 miles down Green Lake Road, going slowly as several camps are located nearly on top of the road. At this point to road continues around the lake, with a dirt road off to the left. As soon as you turn onto the dirt road, there is a parking area on the right.

The Hike: The trailhead indicates that the summit is a mere 0.5 miles away but it is actually just shy of 0.9miles, or 1.7 miles round trip, with an elevation gain of 600 feet. It is considered a moderate hike only because the trail starts out climbing instead of gently introducing itself with a flat grade. The trail is very frequently used, clearly marked and makes for an easy hike for children or slightly out of shape adventurers. The trail itself is part of an old jeep road and has many twists and turns on its' way to the summit. Just prior to reaching the tower, you will pass the former observer's cabin. The summit requires a climb up the fire tower to afford a good view of the area.

Fun Fact: As there are 3 ways to reach the summit, it's possible to do a loop which is a simply 3 mile loop. The North trail isn't nearly as well marked as the other two but still manageable and makes for a fun trek.

LAMPSON FALLS

Getting There: Once in St. Lawrence County, enter the town of Clare, which on the west border of the Adirondack Forest Preserve, and part of the Grass River Wild Forest Preserve. Take County Route 27 out of town approximately 5 miles. Parking is along the side of the road and marked by a DEC sign. If traveling north out of Degrasse, parking will be approximately 4 miles north once you leave town. Note: If coming from Cranberry Lake area, Route 27 is approximately 16-17 miles away from Cranberry Lake when traveling on NY3.

The Hike: Upon exiting your vehicle, pass a gate which symbolizing the start of your hike, which will be along a wide road. At approximately ½ mile, the mail accessible trail branches off to the left with switchbacks taking you through the trees to the falls.   For those choosing to see the falls from the base, there are two ways to get there. A well-worn footpath will get you there but is quite steep, especially if traveling with children. There is also a grassy road/path that will make its' way to the base of the falls as well. This is a short, easy hike that is family friendly and a great place to have a picnic lunch on the beach.

LIMEKILN FALLS

Getting There: From Old Forge, head North on Route 28 toward Inlet. Turn right at the Inlet Golf Course, heading south onto Limekiln Road to the Limekiln Lake Campground entrance. (there is a small fee for day use entrance to the park). The trail can be found near campsite #87.

The Hike: Starting at a large open field at campsite #87, cross the field to find a register box at the old damn, where the nature trail starts. Travel 1.0 miles around the old beaver dam, until the trail bares right after a series of bridges. Continue another ¾ of a mile, following the outlet for Limekiln Lake as the trail crosses over a brook several times before you arrive at the start of the falls. Bring a picnic lunch, and enjoy the view. No worry about being crowded as the falls continue for another ½ mile and you will have plenty of room to spread out.

*This enjoyable hike earns you 2 points on the ADK Waterfall Challenge.

LUDLOWVILLE FALLS

Getting There: From Ithaca, take 34 North out of the city. When 13 and 34 split, take 34 and drive approximately 6 miles north to 34B. Turn left onto NY 34B and drive 2.7 miles. Make a right onto Ludlowville Road, then turn into the parking lot at the Ludlowville Town Park.

The Hike: Once in the park, head toward the fence which is past the playground and the 36 foot falls will spread out in front of you. There is a trail that will take you down to the base of Salmon Creek and reveal the secret cave beside the falls. This is a very short, easy and family friendly hike.

MOSS LAKE LOOP

Getting There: Route 28 North out of Old Forge toward Inlet. Turn left onto Big Moose Road, just north of Eagle Bay. The hike starts at the main parking area off Big Moose Road. Park, sign in, and start your hike counter clockwise around the lake.

The Hike: The entire loop is 2.4 miles in length, with the first part of the loop handicap accessible. Once you reach a large bridge, you've already reached the half way mark. At 1.8 miles, you reach the trail junction with Bubb & Sis Lakes Trail to your right. Shortly after the intersection, you'll cross a large stream on a footbridge.

MOUNT ADAMS

Getting There: Located in Newcomb, this mountain can be accessed from Long Lake or the Northway. From 87, take Exit 29 at North Hudson and head towards Newcomb on Route 28. Approximately 18 or 19 miles later, turn onto Lower Works Road which will become Upper Works Road. Use caution as these roads are heavily traveled as they afford access to the high peaks wilderness area. The parking area will be on the right, just past the McIntyre Iron Works Furnace.

The Hike: Now that there is a new swinging suspension bridge crossing the Hudson, you no longer have to wade through icy water to access the mountain. Once you've crossed the Hudson, you are ready to access the trail to the 3520 foot summit. The official fire tower trail in fact starts just past an abandoned wood shack approx. 10 minutes into your hike. The trail gains 1800 feet of elevation in 1.6 miles of hiking, though none of the areas are very steep, but do in fact demand a few areas of scrambling amongst the rocks. Once you've reached the summit, you will need to climb the firetower to in order to enjoy an amazing vista. Mount Adams is a quick, enjoyable day hike whose views will impress you without leaving you exhausted.

MOUNT ARAB

Getting There: Once in the village of Tupper Lake (north of Long Lake, west of Saranac Lake), turn off Route 30 and onto NY 3 and continue approximately 7 miles west until you come to County Route 62 (Conifer Road). There is a sign on Route 3 indicating Mt Arab once you see signs indicating that you've made it to Piercefield. Take County Road 62 for approximately 1.8 miles to Eagle Crag Lake Road/Mount Arab Road which will be the left. Turn down Eagle Crag Lake Road and continue until you cross rail road tracks. Parking will be on the right 0.3 miles after the tracks.

The Hike: This 2545 foot summit offers amazing views for very little exertion. Barely 2 miles round trip, and will an elevation gain of only 700 feet, this hike is both kid and pet friendly.

MOXHAM MOUNTAIN

Getting There: Route 28 in Minerva to 14th Road. The pavement will end, but continue approximately .2 miles further. Though not a large parking area, you will find a pull off on the left side of the road, with the trail head on the right. Follow the DEC yellow trail markers along your 2.7 mile hike to the summit.

The hike: The trail immediately climbs and offers one of many overlooks just 0.6 miles into the hike. Typical of most ADK hikes, the trail will now start to descend slight and cross a stream. Once over the stream, you will start your accent again. Take a breather at any of the many overlooks that you'll encounter along the trail to the summit. The summit is comprised of mostly open rock and offers spectacular views.

OK SLIP FALLS

Getting There: Easily accessible, OK Slip Falls is located in the Hudson Gorge Wilderness Area and is just 7.5 mile east of the intersection of 30 & 28 in Indian Lake. There is a wooden sign for the Wilderness Area at the parking lot. From the parking area, you need to walk along the highway for 2/10's of a mile and cross the road when you see the trailhead sign. Note: this is the access for several other hikes so the parking might be limited.

The hike: The total round trip mileage to the falls and back is 6.4 miles total. Once you make it to the falls, the trail actually continues 0.8 miles and ends at the Hudson River. The beginning of the trail has many areas that might be muddy, even during the summer season so hiking or waterproof footwear is strongly encouraged. Once past the mud you will be awed by the gorgeous hardwoods, wildflowers and possible wildlife. At the summit, you will find two areas in which to view the waterfalls. The best time to view the falls is in the morning as the falls become shaded by the afternoon.

OSEETAH LAKE

Getting There: Once in Saranac Lake, this adorable lake is conveniently located only a few miles south of the village of Saranac Lake. Located in the town of Harrietstown, this 800 acre lake is shallow despite receiving its' flow from the larger Lower Saranac River.

The Hike: Not so much a hike, but a great lake to drop a canoe or kayak and enjoy an afternoon on the water. But please be respectful of private property and only put in where it's permissible.

OVERLOOK MOUNTAIN

Getting There: Centrally located in the Catskill Mountains, close to Woodstock NY, Overlook Mountain is a quick commute from Route 212 to Rock City Road. Meads Meadow Parking Area is 2 miles down the road on the right.

The Hike: It is only 1.6 miles to the Overlook Mountain House ruins. Formerly the site of an old hotel, its' concrete form offers excellent photo opportunities, but be on the lookout for rattlesnakes that might be sunning themselves amongst the stone ruins. Continue past the ruins and you will quickly reach the summit, which offers amazing views of the Catskill Range.

OWLS HEAD MOUNTAIN

Getting There: This kid and puppy friendly hike is conveniently located just minutes from the village of Lake

Placid, approximately 3.6 miles past the Cascade Mountain trailhead on Route 73, east of the Olympic village (11 miles east, heading towards Keene). Make a right once you see the sign for Owls Head Acres.

The Hike: 1.2 miles round trip, and you will start hiking immediately on an uphill grade. The views are not only fabulous at the summit but also along the way. Make sure you remember your camera as the summit offers stunning views of Hurricane, Pitchoff, Cascade, Porter and Giant. Even though the elevation is only 2120, the views are endless.

OWLS HEAD MOUNTAIN (ANOTHER ONE)

Getting There: From the Intersection of 28 and 30 in Long Lake, follow Route 30 toward Tupper Lake. Turn left in approx. 2 miles onto Endion Road, follow to the end with the trailhead being on the right.

The Hike: The trail is 6.2 miles round trip and I moderately challenging with an summit elevation of 2812, and an elevation gain of 1200 feet. This is a family friendly hike, but give yourself 4-5 hours for the round trip if traveling with children. The trail gradually climbs with the final leg to the summit being very steep with a bit of rock scrambling. One of the ADK's fire towers can be found waiting for you on the summit. Make sure you climb the tower and enjoy the panoramic 360 degree views of the Central Adirondacks and High Peaks Region.

PALMER FALLS

Getting There: From the City of Corinth, Take (N out of town to County Highway 32, northeast of Corinth. Once on 32, you'll find a small parking area on the right.

The Hike: The trail to the Hudson River, and 70 foot Palmer Falls is a quick 3/10's of a mile walk down a well worn trail. The area and nature trails are owned by a Hydroelectric Company, and unfortunately the only time you'll find water coming over their damn, thus creating a "waterfall" is when the water is high. Even though this one won't take your breath away with its' beauty, it's still a fun walk with nature.

PAUL SMITH'S VISITOR INTERPRETIVE CENTER

Getting There: Follow the directions to St. Regis Mountain, or looks for signs 1 mile north of Route 86 & 30 intersection. Paul Smith's is a local college, located just north of Lake Clear in the town of Paul Smiths, and anyone in the area should be able to help you out if you miss a turn.

The Hike: The center offers an amazing butterfly house (during the summer), trails though wetlands on seasoned boardwalks, with many platforms from which to take a rest or a few pictures of the abundant wildlife in the area. There are walking trails through the forest that cover eight miles, along with indoor exhibits, sure to please any nature enthusiast.   In the winter, the trails are used for snowshoeing and cross country skiing.

PILLSBURY MOUNTAIN FIRE TOWER

Getting There: Located 9 miles northwest of Speculator. Take Route 30 North from Speculator approximately 8 miles. Turn left onto a dirt road just past Mason Lake. Follow this dirt road 3.2 miles to junction at Perkins Clearing (marked by a DEC sign). Turn right and end at Sled Harbor, where you will park at Sled Harbor, the Trail Head is a 1.2 mile hike up the road on the right from Sled Harbor. Note: The road is very rough and though it can be driven by most cars, four-wheel drive is preferable.

The Hike: Considered a moderately difficult climb for any out of shape hikers. The 1.5 mile trail climbs nearly 1500 feet from parking to summit. Once on the summit, Snowy Mountain, Siamese Pond Wilderness, along with Lake Pleasant and Sacandaga Lakes can be readily seen to the south. A fun, short hike that will provide a quick workout. This is one of the few fire towers that you will find isn't crowded because of it's out of the way location.

PITCHOFF MOUNTAIN

Getting There: Find your way to Lake Placid. After grabbing some ice cream or a commemorative shirt, follow Route 73out of town, heading toward Keene. Continue for 7.5 miles to the Pitchoff "west" trail. Parking there is also the same as for Cascade Mountain trailhead, so you might want to consider driving another 2.6 miles to the "east" trail.

The Hike: The route climbs steadily above Route 73. You will see Cascade Lake, along with Cascade Mountain along the way. From these lookouts, the trail will become a steeper climb. Thou there is no view from the actual 3600 foot summit, there are plenty of large boulders in which to enjoy your lunch or take a rest.

If you decide to walk the ridge to the East trailhead, the entire trip is 10 miles with an elevation change of 1500 feet. This is a challenging route and not recommended for young children and will take a good portion of your day. Be prepared for a workout.

PIXLEY FALLS

Getting There: From Utica, take either 840 or 49 into Rome, head north out of Rome on Black River Blvd, which becomes 46. The park will be on your right as you head north, approximately 8 miles north of Rome. If coming from the west, get off Thruway at exit 33 to NY 365 East into Rome.

The Hike: HUGE bang for your buck! Great part is, the park is free; so pack your picnic basket and camera and make this a must see! Even though the NY State park is no longer manned by the DEC, the park is still open to the public and has numerous picnic tables and restrooms making your stay very enjoyable! Once in the park, the main, 50-foot waterfall is located within earshot of the picnic area. There is a well-traveled path leading down to the falls, and numerous marked nature trails along the waterway and through the surrounding woods.

POKE-O-MOONSHINE MOUNTAIN

Getting There: Conveniently located just 3 miles from Exit 33 off I-87, on Route 9. The original steep trail still exists and c

an be accessed from the south side of the old campgrounds. If you do the short, steep trail, make sure you go to the right after you see the old chimney. This route rises almost 1300 feet in 1.2 miles.

The hike: If you use the new trail, it is an easier route and kid friendly. The trail is free of rock scrambling and offers many photo ops as you walk past beaver ponds and massive rock ledges. This new trail is one mile south of the old trail and definitely makes for an easier hike. Once on the summit, the panoramic view is truly breathtaking. Lake Champlain is directly to the east, along with several mountains, including Giant, Gothic and Whiteface. As a side note, the fire tower on top of this 2180 foot summit is listed on the National Register of Historic Places.

POTHOLERS FALLS

Getting There: Located in the Ferris Lake Wild Forest in the Adirondack Park, The Potholers is located on the Powley-Piseco Road, on the East Canada Creek. Upon arrival, you'll find plenty of areas on both side of the road to park.

The Hike: It's not much of a strenuous hike, you simply walk to the north side of the culvert where you parked. The trail is unmarked but very well worn and easy to follow. Within 100 or so feet, you'll come across a campsite overlooking the Brayhouse Brook and East Canada. Walk upstream from there and before you know it, you be at Potholers.

Point of Interest: The reason the area is called Potholers is because the rock formation looks like "potholes" in the road. The rocks are soft, rounded and full of hikers cooling off in them during the hot summer months.

RAINBOW FALLS

Getting There: From Cranberry Lake, head out of town on NY 3. Turn onto Tooley Pond Road which will be approximately 11 miles from NY 3. If, by chance, you end up at Tooley Pond, you've gone 5 miles too far but can always stop there to have a picnic. If driving from Cranberry Lake, your clue that you've found the trailhead is a wide stretch of shoulder parking on the right hand side of the road.

The Hike: From your vehicle, the falls are only a 3/10th of a mile walk and very easy to get to. You will note boulders on the old dirt road preventing motor vehicles. A word of caution though; if traveling with small children, please keep them close as the viewing area can be slippery and steep, with fast moving water below.

RED HILL FIRE TOWER

Getting There: Directions from the Thruway is the easiest route, but not the shortest. Take exit 19 off the Thruway (Kingston exit). Take Route 28 West for ½ mile, then right onto Rt 209 towards Ellenville. Continue on Route 209 for 24.6 miles, then turn right onto Route 55. Continue another 16 miles on Route 55. Finally turn right again onto route 19 and go another 6.4 miles until you reach Red Hill Road. Once on Red Hill Road. Go 3.2 miles before taking a left onto Coons Road. Finally, 1.1 miles up Coons, you will find the DEC parking lot on the left side.

The Hike: One of the easiest hikes in the Catskills, the walk to the summit is only 1.42 miles long and is not difficult nor steep. There are picnic table on the summit so make sure you remember to bring a lunch. Average hiking enthusiasts take approximately 2.5 hours to make the round trip. With an elevation gain of only 996 feet, this is a great hike for kids, and pets alike.

*Note: This summit is one of 5 required Fire towers in the Catskills, and part of the NY State Fire tower Challenge.

REMSEN FALLS

Getting There: From Utica, head North on Route 12 to Route 28 North. Just past the town of Otter Lake, look for Mckeever Road on the right (before you cross over the Moose River Bridge). Take McKeever Road past the old train station and continue until you see the trail information board at the parking area. The sign will say "Remsen Falls Forest Preserve"

The Hike: The hike to the falls is a ADK flat 3.5 mile hike but well worth your time and effort. On a side note, this trails has a tendency to be muddy so wear waterproof footwear.

ROCK LAKE & ROCK RIVER

Getting There: Located in the Blue Mountain Wild Forest, both trailheads are located on Route 28/30 and each have a small parking area. From Lake Durant State Campground, head east on NY 28/30. Both trailheads can be found on the north side of the road, with Rock Lake Trail parking area first.

The Hike: The Rock Lake Trail is less than a mile to the shore of Rock Lake. It is a very easy, kid friendly trail. The Rock River Trail is 3 miles to the banks of the Rock River, where there is an old campsite. If you don't have the energy to climb Blue Mountain, then bring your lunch and hike back to this quiet, less traveled lake.

ROCKWELL FALLS

Getting there: The falls are located close to the hamlet of Lake Lazerne. Take 9N off the Northway to Lake Luzerne. Head west on Route 4 out of town. The falls are next to where the Sacandaga River joins the Hudson River, just outside of town.

The Hike: The falls are located a short walk upstream where the Sacandaga River meets with the Hudson River. This is a waterfall hike that requires absolutely no effort and can actually be viewed from the bridge as you cross over the Hudson River. Park alongside the road, being wary of passing vehicles, and cross the bridge for the best view of the falls.

ROCKY FALLS

Getting There: Located near Lake Placid, the trailhead can be found on the Adirondack Loj Road. There is a huge parking area that can accommodate the considerable number of hikers that flock to this area every summer. From the intersection of 73 & 86 in Lake Placid, take Route 73 out of town, heading towards Keene. Continue until you see the Adirondack Loj Road on your right-hand side.

The Hike: This family friendly hike is less than five miles round trip. From the parking area, cross the road and this is where your adventure begins. (keep in mind that the numerous cars in the parking lot aren't all venturing towards the falls. This is the access for hikers climbing Mount Jo and the trail for Indian Pass). Once on the trail, continue toward Indian Pass. You will be walking on a well-worn, ADK flat path and quickly will come to the trail for Rocky Falls on your right. The falls are moments away.

SAND LAKE FALLS

Getting There: From Utica, take 12 North to 28 North in Alder Creek. In Woodgate, turn right off 28 onto Bear Creek Road (look for the blinking light, and sign to left indicating road to Boonville). Drive down Bear Creek Road to the large parking lot on the left. From here, there is a rough road known as Mill Creek road. It is recommended that you walk, or bike this road, and vehicles are discouraged.

The Hike: From the parking lot, you will walk/jog/bike approx. 2.2 miles before coming to a four way intersection. The trail to the right leads to Gull Lake Trail, and the trail on the left is part of the Bear Creek trail. Continue straight and at approximately 3.4 miles, you'll reach the end of Mill Creek Road. The Sand Lake Falls Trail continues straight from here. Be on the lookout for the DEC markers indicating that you'll still following the old woods trail. It'll take 6.4 miles before the trails reaches the Sand Lake Falls lean to. Take a quick breather, and follow the trail another 100 feet and you will find what you've been searching for, Sand Lake Falls!

SAWYER MOUNTAIN TRAIL

Getting There: Located close to trailheads of Rock Lake and Rock River Trail, take Route 28/30 from Lake Durant State Campground in Blue Mountain and look for the DEC sign. If leaving from Indian Lake Village, the trailhead is northwest of the village on 28.

The Hike: This is a one mile moderate hike to the summit, in the Blue Ridge Wilderness area. Many combine this easy, quick hike with the trail back to Rock Lake and Rock River.

SCARFACE MOUTAIN

Getting There: In Saranac Lake, head toward Lake Placid on Route 86. Once you enter Ray Brook, take a right onto Ray Brook Road and the trailhead will be on the left in 1/10 of a mile.

The Hike: This 6.8 round trip hike offers something for everyone. Gorgeous vegetation to photo opportunities, steep terrain for scrambling over, and Ray Brook for anyone interested in doing a little fishing along the way. As you cross over a bridge crossing Ray Brook and the road splits, be sure and take the left trail to the summit. When you reach the summit, and even beforehand, you'll have plenty of opportunities to take great pictures on one of the landings along the way.

SHELVING ROCK FALLS AND MOUNTAIN

Getting There: Adirondack Northway to exit 20. Route 9 East, past the outlet malls. Turn right onto Route 149 east until you see the sign for Buttermilk Falls Road on your left (approximately 5.8 miles). Continue down Buttermilk Falls Road to Sly Pond Road to Shelving Rock Road. The road is the same, it just changes names along the approximately 11 mile stretch. You will end up at the Hog Town Parking Lot. Take a left at this parking lot and the trailhead is approximately 2.7 miles on your right. To the falls: While on Shelving Rock Road, you will see an orange painted steel gate. The trail starts there. This easy day hike is 2.0 miles round trip if you continue past the falls, down to the lake. Pack a lunch and enjoy this family friendly jaunt.

SINCLAIR FALLS

Getting There: From Cranberry Lake, take NY3 out of town until you intersect Tooley Pond Road. The parking lot will be found shortly after the intersection of Tooley Pond Road and Lake George Road.

The Hike: You will find a herd path descending from the parking lot and within a minute or two, you will reach the falls. If you feel that this trail, though short, is too steep for you, then there is an alternative. The second trail to the falls is located along Lake George Road, just before the bridge that crosses the Grass River. Here you will find a small parking area.

SPLIT ROCK FALLS

Getting There: From the Northway, take exit 30 onto Route 73 Northwest, to Route 9 North. The series of falls is part of the Bouquet River. There is a parking area off 9 but the falls are unmarked, so look for a parking lot with a large fence.

The Hike: It can't really be called a hike, as the falls are very close to the road. From the parking lot, head towards the fence and go to your left. At the end of the fence, there will be a well-worn trail through the trees to a decent sized ledge to view the falls.

SPRUCE MOUNTAIN

Getting There: Located in the town of Corinth, the trailhead is a snowplow turnaround at the end of Spruce Mountain Road, off Wells Road, in South Corinth.

The Hike: Kind of a noneventful hike, is accessible by a service road, approx. 1.2miles in length. The area was logged in the past and remains of the past logging operations are evident as you walk on the trail. The hike might get your heart pumping as it has an elevation gain of 1011 in this 1.2 mile hike.

Note: There are no views from the summit and the tower is closed. BUT, if you're working on your ADK fire tower challenge, Spruce is an easy one to add to your list.

SQUAW BROOK FALLS

Getting There: From Indian Lake, head south on Route 30. Approximately 3.4 miles out of town, you will come to a small bridge. The falls lies between the road and Indian Lake, to the east of the road.

The Hike: There is no like, per say. The falls and gorge can be viewed from the bridge and the land surround the falls is private, so please don't trespass.

*Note: Taking the time to enjoy this adorable roadside waterfall, earns you 1 point on the ADK Waterfall Challenge.

ST REGIS MOUNTAIN

Getting There: From Tupper Lake or Saranac Lake, Take Route 30 to Paul Smiths. Turn left onto Keese Mills Road at the NY Route 86 Junction. The trail head is on the left in approximately 2 miles, west of Paul Smiths.

The Hike: As an author, I know I need to be non-biased, but THIS HIKE IS MY FAVORITE FIRE TOWER OF THE FIRE TOWER CHALLENGE. The trail is a 3.3 mile accent to the summit. During the hike, the elevation gain is 1168 feet to the summit. But, the view from the summit offers 30 lakes, and many high peaks. This summit truly offers a panoramic view and is bare rock so you can sit anywhere to enjoy the view and your lunch.

TENANT CREEK FALLS

Getting There: These 3 falls are located within the Wilcox Lake Wild Forest preserve. From Northville, take Route 30 North until you see Old Northville Road. Turn right on Old Northville Road. Drive approximately 1.4 miles, and turn left onto Hope Falls Road. From there, drive approximately 7 miles on Hope Falls Road. Don't be dismayed when the last mile of the road is dirt; you are still heading the right way. There will be a large parking lot, located on the right.

The Hike: This is a great one with children since you can complete your journey to a waterfalls in less than a mile. The first waterfalls is 9/10's of a mile from the parking lot, while the 2nd and 3 waterfalls are only a little over 2 miles away. At 0.8 miles, you'll cross a small stream, but this is not what you're in search of. Just a little farther up the trail, you'll find Tenant Creek and your first waterfall.

TREMPER MOUNTAIN AND FIRETOWER

Getting There: From the thruway take Exit 20 (Saugerties) to 32 South. Then a quick right onto Route 212 at the red light. Take Route 212 9 miles into Woodstock. Continue 1.8 miles to Brearsville, then right toward Phoenicia.

Continue on Route 212 for another 9.2 miles, then take a right onto Route 40. Take 2 miles to DEC Parking lot on the right.

The Hike: With an elevation gain of nearly 2000 feet (1966 to be exact), Tremper's summit elevation is 2724. The hike is an easy walk, with limited views from the fire tower on the summit.

Note: Don't wander too close to the blue stone quarry half way up the trail, unless you like timber rattlers. It is reported that there are approximately 100+ timber rattlesnakes in the den in the quarry, and caution is advised.

*This hike is part of the ADK Fire Tower Challenge, and one of the 5 mandatory Catskill Fire Towers.

VANDERWHACKER MOUNTAIN

Getting There: From 28/30 in Old Forge, head north to Blue Mountain. Just before the Blue Mountain Museum, bare Right onto 28 East toward Indian Lake. Just prior to crossing the Boreas River, there is a DEC sign and gravel road to the right. Take this unmarked road approx. 2.6 miles to the point where it splits. Parking is on the right. The road can be very rough, so drive slow and use caution as it becomes quite narrow.

The Hike: This family friendly hike offers something for everyone. The beginning of the hike is a slow ascend, on a trail that has you crossing several creeks, wetlands, and massive trees. Once you get a mile in, the trail splits. If you are hiking to the summit, you need to bare right as the trail to the left is the old road, and now utilized as a snowmobile trail in the winter. After the split, you will encounter two cabins used formerly as observer's cabins. From here, the climb becomes more strenuous. The total elevation gain is over 1650 feet with majority of it during that last half of the hike. Take your time, catch your breath and make it to the summit. You won't be disappointed. Though the summit is partially obscured, the views from the top of the tower offer a panoramic 360 view of the high peaks.

Note: This hike is part of the Fire tower Challenge and one of the more enjoyable climbs in the area. Even though the summit is only 3386 feet, this one gives you better views than many of the true "high peaks".

WATCH HILL

Use the same directions as you would for Snowy Mountain, be on the lookout for a parking area on the opposite side of the road (heading south, it'll be on your left).

The Hike: This is a very family friendly hike, and makes for a short walk with bountiful views; and an excellent place to have a picnic along the shores of Indian Lake. Once in the woods, the trails' a woods road for the first 7/10 of a mile. Make sure at this point you follow the trail at the signed intersection to the summit. The grade is slightly steeper at this point. After a few minutes, you'll come to a large ledge offering majestic views, but don't stop there. Continue walking down a slight descent to another viewpoint. At this juncture, you can choose to walk down another 7/10ths of a mile to the shore of Indian Lake and have a picnic or cast a fishing rod. Upon your return, please note that the hike from the lake back to the trail head ascends over 400 feet quickly and might require a few rest breaks. If Watch Hill makes your list, make sure you're on the lookout for Snowy Mountain as you climb, as it's directly across the road from your trail.

WATKINS GLEN

Getting There: Located in the southernmost part of Seneca Lake, the main entrance can be found off NY State 14, in Watkins Glen proper. The southern entrance to the Glen can be found off NY State 329.

The Hike: Wear comfortable shoes and in peak summer season, bring a water bottle and your patience as the Gorge trails can be packed with other fellow visitors. The Park itself is one of the most recognizable and popular parks in all of New York State and well worth the drive to the finger lakes region. There are 3 main park trails, each offers amazing vistas as they wind their way throughout the gorge. They are named the Indian trail, Gorge trail and Southern Rim trail. If you don't mind getting just a little wet from the waterfall's spray, then the Gorge Trail is a must. It not only brings you over the waterfalls but under it as well. The Rim trail will remind you of the Grand Canyon as it overlooks the Gorge, and for the thrill seeker, the Indian Trail will have you suspended high above the Gorge as you cross it on a suspension bridge!

WAKELY MOUNTAIN

Getting There: From Indian Lake, head approx. two miles west out of town. Turn left onto Cedar River Road, and then proceed approximately 12 miles. The pavement ends but you keep going. The parking area is on the right and there is a sign marking the trail. If somehow you miss it, and continue on the road, you will see a barrier and markings for the Northville-Placid Trail and path to Wakely Dam.

The Hike: This 6 mile round trip is quite level for the beginning half, then steep for the remainder. (Don't make the mistake we did, and park in the wrong parking lot, or you will add an additional 9+ miles to your hike). The summit of Wakely is so close to being a "high peak", with an elevation of 3744 feet. You will see an elevation gain of nearly 1200 within the first mile. From the trailhead, your journey will start along a gravel road, with the road paralleling a stream in the beginning. You will cross a few streams before you see a sign to your right points you in the direction of the direct path to the summit and fire tower. Make sure when you reach the summit you climb the fire tower as it will provide you the only 360 degree views, including Snowy and Blue Mountain.

Note: This awesome hike is part of the Fire tower Challenge.

WHETSTONE GULF STATE PARK

Getting There: Located at 6056 West Road, Lowville; this 2100 acre state park is located in Lewis County off Route 12. On the edge of the Tug Hill plateau, it is just south of Lowville, and north of Turin NY.

The Hike: the 4.5 mile loop within the park makes for spectacular views of a three mile long glacial gorge and comes complete with observation platform, plenty of picnic areas, and a very easy family friendly trail. The elevation gain is only 892 feet so you won't work up a sweat. Grab the kids, your camera and a lunch, and head on over to Lewis County today. You won't be disappointed!

WHISKEY BROOK FALLS

Getting There: Situated 2 miles north of Speculator, drive 2.2 miles North on Route 30. Look off to the right for the stream that crosses under the road. Immediately pull off, park.

The Hike: This very small and easily accessible falls is only 50 feet from where you parked, on the eastern side of the road. Bring a lunch and enjoy the serenity while surrounded by large boulders.

*Note: This short stroll counts towards 1 point of your ADK Waterfall Challenge.

WOODHULL MOUNTAIN

Getting There: Located just 6 miles south of Old Forge off Route 28, this fun mountain offers a little something for everyone. For the biking enthusiast, your journey begins from the parking lot. From 28, take McKeever Road just past the Moose River. Continue down the gravel road once the blacktop ends. You will see a parking lot on the right; continue down the gravel road. When the road splits, remain on the jeep road to the right, and continue another 3 miles until you see a small State Parking lot on the left. There is a gated woods road that leads to the trailhead.

The Hike: This fire tower hike is one of the less populated hikes you will experience, and I'm not exactly sure why. Bikers have an advantage over hikers as they can bike the first few miles in as the trail is flat, and an old logging trail. The elevation change is minimal for an Adirondack Mountain, with it being only 812 feet. Most reference books label this hike as difficult, not because of the climb, but the distance one has to hike to get to the summit. But don't let that dissuade you from climbing this short but sweet mountain. Bring a picnic lunch and enjoy eating at one of the picnic tables along the Moose River when you're done. And if you're still looking for more hiking, make sure you walk the half mile down to Remsen Falls while you're at it.

Note: This hike is part of the ADK Firetower Challenge.

I sincerely hope that you find this little "guidebook" a stepping stone towards your exploration of our beautiful outdoors.

Hikes don't have to be miles in length, or hours of scrambling up rocks, boulders and cliffs. Any time you venture off the couch, you're already winning the game. Children are like sponges; they'll absorb whatever they're exposed to, be it a day hike to a fishing hole, or a picnic alongside a waterfalls. No child is too young to start learning about our wonderful planet and even though they are just outside for the adventure of it, you are teaching them so much more than any TV show or game on their phone could ever teach them. Time spent with our children is the precious gift that we can give them. And if you don't have children, our four legged friends will be just as appreciative if they're included as well.

~~~See you on the trails~~~

Made in the USA
Monee, IL
15 October 2023